Burr Elementary School
1960 Burr Street
Fairfield, CT 06824

A Picture Book of
John Hancock

by David A. Adler and Michael S. Adler
illustrated by Ronald Himler

Holiday House / New York

For my grandson, Jacob
D. A. A.

For my son, Jacob
M. S. A.

Text copyright © 2007 by David A. Adler and Michael S. Adler
Illustrations copyright © 2007 by Ronald Himler
All Rights Reserved
Printed in the United States of America
www.holidayhouse.com
First Edition
1 3 5 7 9 10 8 6 4 2

Library of Congress Cataloging-in-Publication Data

Adler, David A.
A picture book of John Hancock / by David A. Adler and Michael S. Adler ;
illustrated by Ronald Himler.— 1st ed.
p. cm.
Includes bibliographical references.
ISBN-13: 978-0-8234-2005-6 (hardcover)
ISBN-10: 0-8234-2005-1 (hardcover)
1. Hancock, John, 1737–1793—Juvenile literature. 2. Statesmen—United States—Biography—Juvenile
literature. 3. United States. Declaration of Independence—Signers—Biography—Juvenile literature.
4. United States—History—Revolution, 1775–1783—Juvenile literature. I. Adler, Michael S. II. Himler,
Ronald, ill. III. Title.

E302.6.H23A35 2007
973.3'092—dc22
[B]
2005052649

The Declaration of Independence was an act of defiance. It accused England's King George III of tyranny. On July 4, 1776, John Hancock boldly signed the Declaration. He signed it large enough, he said, so "George the Third can read *that* without his spectacles."

John Hancock was born on January 12, 1737, in Braintree (now Quincy), Massachusetts. He was the second of three children born to the Reverend John and Mary Hancock. John spent his early years listening to his father's sermons in church. He also played with friends. One of those friends was John Adams, the future president of the United States.

When John Hancock was seven, his father died. His mother was afraid she could not afford to raise all her children, so she split up the family. John was sent to live with his childless aunt and uncle, Lydia and Thomas Hancock, in their mansion on Beacon Hill, then a suburb of Boston.

John's wealthy aunt and uncle gave him the best education available. He was taught at home until he was eight, then sent to the Boston Public Latin School and later went to Harvard College. After graduation he worked for his uncle's company. He "became an example to all the young men of the town," John Adams later wrote. "He was regular and punctual at his store as the sun in his course."

In 1760 Thomas Hancock sent John to London for a year to work.

London was the largest city in Europe. It had many shops and theaters. It was an exciting place to be. It also had a new king, George III. Still, John Hancock was anxious to go home. He missed his friends in America.

In October 1761 he returned to Boston. Three years later his uncle died. At twenty-four John Hancock became one of the wealthiest men in the American colonies.

In 1765 the new king and the British parliament passed the Stamp Act, a tax on many items sent to the American colonies, including ships' papers, playing cards, and dice. It was passed to help pay the huge debt caused by the French and Indian War.

Both as a businessman and a patriot, John Hancock hated the Stamp Act. Other colonists did too. In May 1766 Parliament repealed it. But soon Parliament passed the Townshend Acts, which taxed glass, lead, paint, paper, and tea.

On April 8, 1768, John and a small group of patriots refused to allow customs officials onto one of Hancock's ships to collect the new taxes. Two months later a customs official boarded another of Hancock's boats. The official was held by the captain while the cargo was unloaded. The next day the British navy took the ship.

Britain's harsh rule and the new taxes angered many colonists. On March 5, 1770, colonists shouted at British soldiers. The soldiers fired into the crowd, killing five men. That act came to be known as the Boston Massacre.

On June 9, 1772, off Rhode Island, patriots burned a Royal Navy ship, the *Gaspee*. On December 16, 1773, in an act known as the Boston Tea Party, patriots dumped thousands of pounds of British tea into the harbor.

The British responded by passing the Coercive Acts. Town meetings were no longer allowed. Boston Harbor was closed.

Some colonial leaders still hoped the two sides could be brought together, but not Hancock. What use is law, he wondered, "when administered by tyrants who violate it themselves?"

In 1774 Hancock joined the local committee of correspondence. This was one of many such groups that informed people about what was happening elsewhere in the colonies. These groups helped to unify the colonies and to rally them against the British.

On September 5 Hancock went to Philadelphia as a delegate to the First Continental Congress. There was talk of the colonies getting ready to fight for the right to govern themselves.

In October Hancock was elected president of the new Massachusetts government. Under his leadership, weapons were collected and stored in Concord. Mills were set up to make gunpowder. Bands of minutemen— men ready to fight at a minute's notice—were formed.

In April 1775 King George III ordered the arrest of the biggest troublemakers. To the British that meant John Hancock and Samuel Adams, who were in Lexington, Massachusetts, at the time. British soldiers were sent to Lexington with orders to capture the two men. Then they were to go to nearby Concord and destroy the rebels' weapons. Paul Revere and William Dawes rode from Boston to warn the patriots. The British were coming!

It was almost daybreak on April 19 when Hancock, Adams, and Hancock's friend Dorothy "Dolly" Quincy left Lexington. On their way they heard the sounds of fifes, and drums, and the British marching. A short while later they heard the first shots of the Revolutionary War. Adams remarked, "What a glorious morning is this!"

In May 1775 when the Second Continental Congress met, John Hancock was elected its president. Colonel George Washington was selected to lead the newly formed Continental army. The delegates talked about independence.

Three months later, on August 28, 1775, John Hancock married Dolly, who was ten years his junior. They were to have two children, Lydia and John. Neither child lived to adulthood.

Hancock returned to the congress in the spring of 1776. On June 28 a draft of the Declaration of Independence was presented. It declared, "These United Colonies are, and of Right ought to be Free and Independent States." On July 4, 1776, John Hancock, as president of the congress, became the first man to sign it.

John Hancock stayed a member of the congress until 1778. Then he left to take command of the Massachusetts militia. In 1780 he was elected the first governor of Massachusetts.

On October 19, 1781, British General Charles Lord Cornwallis surrendered to George Washington at Yorktown. This was the last great battle of the Revolution. Two years later, in Paris, France, representatives of the United States signed a treaty of peace. Now the young nation Governor Hancock helped lead was truly independent.

In 1788 he was elected president of the Massachusetts State Convention. Even though he was ill, he successfully pushed for Massachusetts to approve the new federal Constitution.

On October 8, 1793, while still governor, John Hancock died. More than twenty thousand people attended his funeral, including his boyhood friend Vice President John Adams. *The Chronicle*, a newspaper of the time, reported "a general gloom was visible" on every face.

During the Revolution, when Boston was held by the British, patriots destroyed much of the city. "Although I am probably the largest property-owner," Hancock said, "I am anxious the thing should be done if it will benefit the cause."

John Hancock was always ready to risk his great wealth for the public good. He was devoted to service, liberty, and the new nation he had helped to start.

IMPORTANT DATES

1737   Born in Braintree, Massachusetts, January 12.

1744   After father dies, is sent to live with Thomas and Lydia Hancock.

1754   Graduates Harvard College.

1764   Upon death of his uncle, becomes one of the wealthiest merchants in America.

1765   Stamp Act is passed.

1766   Elected to Massachusetts General Assembly.

1770   Boston Massacre, March 5.

1773   Boston Tea Party, December 16.

1774   First Continental Congress convenes, September 5.

1775   Barely escapes from Lexington at start of Revolutionary War, April 19.

        Becomes president of Second Continental Congress, May 5.

        Marries Dorothy "Dolly" Quincy, August 28.

1776   Signs Declaration of Independence, July 4.

1778   Heads the Massachusetts militia.

1780   Elected governor of Massachusetts.

1783   England recognizes the new nation.

1793   Dies in Boston, October 8.

SOURCE NOTES

Each source note includes the first word or words and the last word or words of a quotation and its source. References are to books cited in the Selected Bibliography.

"George . . . without his spectacles.": Brown, p. 211.

"became an example . . . in his course.":
Allan, p. 60.

"when administered . . . it themselves?":
Musick, p. 49.

"What . . . is this!": Sears, p. 166.

"a general gloom was visible":
Allan, pp. 359–360.

"Although I am . . . benefit the cause.":
Musick, p. 157.

SELECTED BIBLIOGRAPHY

Allan, Herbert S. *John Hancock: Patriot in Purple*. New York: Beechurst Press, 1953.

Brown, Abraham English. *John Hancock: His Book*. Boston: Lee and Shepard, 1898.

Musick, John R. *John Hancock: A Character Sketch*. Milwaukee: H. G. Campbell Publishing, 1903.

Sears, Lorenzo. *John Hancock: The Picturesque Patriot*. Boston: Little, Brown, 1912.

Umbreit, Kenneth Bernard. *Founding Fathers: Men Who Shaped Our Tradition*. New York: Kennikat Press, 1941.

Ungar, Harlow Giles. *John Hancock: Merchant King and American Patriot*. New York: John Wiley & Sons, 2000.

RECOMMENDED WEBSITES

www.ushistory.org/declaration/signers/hancock.htm

www.americaslibrary.org/cgi-bin/page.cgi/jb/colonial/hancock_1

www.johnhancock.org

AUTHORS' NOTES

In 1819 Thomas Jefferson wrote that every delegate but John Dickinson was at the July 4, 1776, signing of the Declaration of Independence. But because copies exist with only the signatures of Hancock and House Secretary Charles Thomson, some scholars have concluded that only those two were present.

Shortly after being elected president of the United States, George Washington toured the nation. Upon his arrival in Massachusetts, state and local delegates met him, but not the governor, John Hancock, allegedly because he was suffering from gout. Washington took offense at the snub, not to him but to the office of president, and commented, "Had I anticipated it, I would have avoided the place."